Heritage Of Harmony

Celebrating the Threads that Bind Us
Together

Shashikala Gundlupet

BookLeaf
Publishing

India | USA | UK

Made with ❤ on the BookLeaf Publishing Platform
www.bookleafpub.in
www.bookleafpub.com

Dedication

This book is dedicated to the vibrant tapestry of cultures, languages, and traditions that together form the essence of our nation. To the individuals and communities who embrace their unique identities while cultivating bonds of friendship and understanding, your stories and spirit inspire us all.

May this collection serve as a celebration of our shared humanity, reminding us that our diversity is not a barrier, but a bridge that connects us. Let us cherish the rich heritage that flourishes in our differences and continues to shape our journey together. Together, may we honor the past and pave the way for a future built on unity, respect, and love.

Preface

Preface

In a world that often highlights differences, it is crucial to take a moment to celebrate the beauty found in our shared heritage. "Heritage of Harmony" is a poetic exploration of the intricate mosaic that defines our society—a mosaic made up of countless cultures, languages, and traditions that coexist and flourish together.

Within these pages, you will find reflections inspired by the vibrant festivals that light up the calendar, the rich histories that echo through our streets, and the everyday interactions that weave the fabric of our communal life. Each poem serves as a reminder that while we may come from various backgrounds, our hearts beat as one, united in the pursuit of love, understanding, and empathy.

This collection invites readers to embrace the concept of unity in diversity, encouraging us to foster connections and appreciate the unique experiences that each individual brings to our shared table. The poems seek to capture moments of joy, resilience, and the profound connections we can build when we honor one another's stories.

As you journey through these verses, may you feel inspired to celebrate the richness of our collective identity and embrace the harmony that arises from our differences. Together, let us cultivate a world where every voice is heard, every culture is respected, and every person is valued.

Welcome to "Heritage of Harmony."

Acknowledgements

I would like to express my heartfelt gratitude to those who have supported me throughout this journey of writing my book.

A special thank you to my husband, Vaidyanatha, for your unwavering support and encouragement. Your belief in me has been a source of strength. To my daughter, Gargi, thank you for being my inspiration and joy.

I am deeply grateful to my mother, Pushpa, for instilling in me a love for literature and learning. To my mother-in-law, Lakshmi, and my father-in-law, Venkataramu, your guidance and wisdom have played a vital role in my life.

I would also like to extend my appreciation to Mrs. Malati Kalmadi, the secretary of the Kannada Sangha, for your invaluable support and encouragement. To Mrs. Sumathi Srinivasan, Dr. Sameena Manasawa, and Mrs. Reshma Deshpande, thank you for your insights and help in shaping my work.

Lastly, to my wonderful office colleagues, thank you for

your camaraderie and support during this endeavor.
Each of you has contributed to this book in unique ways,
and I am truly grateful.

Thank you all from the bottom of
my heart.

1. Unity in Diversity

In a land where rivers flow like dreams,
A tapestry of colors, bursting at the seams.
Languages dance, each voice a song,
In the heart of our nation, we all belong.

From snow-capped peaks to the sunlit sands,
Different cultures, like grains in our hands.
Festivals rise with the dawn's gentle light,
A chorus of laughter, a beautiful sight.

In every market, scents of spice blend,
Traditions entwine, on this we depend.
A Hindu prayer, a Mosque's call to prayer,
A Christian hymn floats softly in the air.

Footprints of ancients guide us today,
Through history's pages, we find our way.
In unity's embrace, we stand proud and tall,
For in our diversity, we cherish it all.

In the colors of rangoli, stories unfold,
Of legends and myths, of young and of old.
Each dance tells a story, each song sings a truth,
A celebration of life in the spirit of youth.

Across the fields where the farmers toil,
Or bustling streets where the dreams uncoil,
Every artisan crafts with a loving hand,
Creating a masterpiece from every strand.

The warmth of a smile, the share of a meal,
In the simplest moments, our connections feel real.
A cup of chai, a shared laugh or tear,
In these fleeting instances, we draw ever near.

Together we rise, through storm and through sun,
Celebrating each heart, every race, everyone.
Hand in hand, we weave our fate,
In this vibrant mosaic, we all celebrate.

So let us together embrace what is true,
In our differences, find strength anew.
For in this grand journey, as one we shall strive,
In the unity of diversity, we truly thrive.

2. Songs of Sacred Earth

In twilight's glow, the sacred earth does sing,
A harmony of life in every hue,
Where rivers flow and ancient mountains cling,
And whispers tell of wonders ever true.

The rustling leaves compose a gentle tune,
Each breeze, a messenger of tales untold,
Beneath the stars, beneath the silver moon,
The spirit of the wild and bold unfolds.

With every dawn, the flowers wake and bloom,
In fields adorned with colors pure and bright,
Their scent, a fragrant breath that banishes gloom,
Restoring hope and joy within our sight.

So let us pause, in nature's arms to dwell,
And hear the songs of earth, a sacred spell.

In every grain of soil, life finds its worth,
A tapestry of voices, intertwined,

For in our hearts, we carry sacred earth,
A bond of love and peace, forever blind.

May we protect this treasure, pure and rare,
And join the song—our planet's heartfelt prayer

3. Threads of Tradition

In a small village, where the sun kissed the earth,
An old woman sat by her window,
Her hands busy with a loom that sang,
A melody of generations past.
Each thread she wove was a tale,
Of laughter, of sorrow, of love,
A vibrant tapestry capturing moments,
In colors that shimmered like life's emotions.

Her granddaughter, eyes wide with curiosity,
Approached and asked, "Grandma, tell me the tale,
Of how the threads of our family intertwine."
With a smile, the elder began,
"Once, my dear, on the banks of the sacred Ganges,
Our ancestors gathered to celebrate life,
Every festival was a thread spun from joy,
We danced in the rain, painted our hearts with colors,
And sang songs that echoed through the valleys."

"Remember Holi? The riot of colors,

Where laughter blended with the fragrance of blossoms,
In every splash of pink and yellow,
We lost ourselves, became one with the earth,
Tradition wrapped us in vibrant hues,
Binding our spirits in joyous embrace."

She paused, eyes glimmering like the setting sun,
"On Diwali nights, we adorned our homes with lights,
Every diya flickered with hope,
A reminder that even in darkness,
The light of love prevails,
And we share stories under the stars,
Passing wisdom like an heirloom."

The little girl, filled with wonder, replied,
"But what about the flavors, Grandma?
The spices that dance in our kitchens?"
A laugh erupted from the old woman's lips,
"Ah, my child, cooking is an art,
A language of love spoken through spices,
Each meal a tradition, gathered around a table,
From fragrant biryanis to sweet laddoos,
Every bite tells our history,
Rich with the laughter of family gathered close."

As the sun set behind the hills,
The children played outside, their laughter echoing,

While the grandmother continued her weaving,
The loom a constant rhythm, like her heartbeat,
Each cross of thread weaving the family's story,
Binding them in a legacy of resilience and hope.

"You see, my dear, tradition is not just the past,
It is the present we live, the future we weave,
In every gathering, every feast, every song,
We affirm our identity, our roots and our dreams,
Stronger together, like the fabric of our lives,
With love as the thread that holds us all."

And as night fell, the stars twinkling overhead,
The village slept, wrapped in the warmth of tradition,
A colorful quilt of stories, passed on and embraced,
For in the threads of tradition, they found their unity,
A legacy flowing through time, forever intertwined.

4. Festival of Colours

In the air, a whisper of spring,
Joy dances upon the breeze,
As the sun smiles down on the earth,
The world awakens, vibrant and free.

Children gather, laughter fills the streets,
Armed with bags of colors, a rainbow in hand,
With every splash, a burst of delight,
Each hue a memory, a bond that expands.

Red for the love that blossoms anew,
Yellow for warmth, like sun's embrace,
Blue for the joy that dances in the heart,
Green for the laughter that knows no pace.

Water balloons take flight in the air,
A symphony of giggles, splashes, and cheer,
Friends and families, united in play,
Painting their lives as the festival draws near.

Sweets share the sweetness of friendship and love,
Gulab jamun glistens, each bite brings a smile,
As colors blend, worries fade,
In this moment, hearts rejoice for a while.

In the evening, under skies painted dusk,
Bonfires flicker, stories weave through the night,
As the colors of the day begin to settle,
Their beauty lingers, soft and bright.

Holi, a reminder of life's canvas,
Where every shade tells a tale of its own,
Let us embrace the joy, the laughter, the light,
In the festival of colors, we find our home.

5. Echoes of faith

Amidst the whispers of a quiet dawn,
Faith lingers in the spaces between breaths,
A gentle murmur, a soft assurance,
That grounds the soul as heavy doubts arise.

In every shadow, a flicker of light,
Stories etched in the fabric of our hearts,
We gather fragments of hope like stardust,
Each echo a reminder of the strength we hold.

Through stormy nights when courage wavers,
Echoes of faith cradle our weary minds,
They weave the past with threads of tomorrow,
Binding the lost to a vision of what can be.

In laughter shared and tears that flow freely,
In moments of silence, the truth unfolds,
Faith invites us to dance in the uncertainty,
To take bold steps into the great unknown.

The world may shift, seasons may change,
But the echoes remain, steadfast and clear,
A chorus of resilience, love unending,
Guiding us home, wherever we roam.

So listen closely, as the heart beats soft,
In each echo, a promise that whispers,
You are not alone in this journey of life—
Faith echoes through the chambers of our being

6. Harmony in Handoven textiles

In villages where the rivers run clear,
Artisans work with patience and cheer,
Their looms a sanctuary of color and thread,
Where dreams are spun, and visions are spread.

With every shuttle's passage, a story unfolds,
Of cultures entwined in the fibers they hold,
Patterns like whispers of lands far away,
Echoing traditions that never decay.

From markets bustling with laughter and life,
To quiet homes filled with warmth and strife,
Handwoven textiles tell tales of the heart,
Of journeys begun, and of times set apart.

Embroidered with symbols of hope and of grace,
Each piece carries whispers of time and space,
A blanket of comfort, a tapestry bright,
A bridge connecting our worlds, day and night.

As firelight dances on fabric adorned,
You feel the embrace of the gathered and worn,
The harmony sings through each fold and each seam,
A celebration of spirit, a woven dream.

So let us honor the craft that they share,
The weavers of stories, the artists who care,
For in every textile, a legacy flows,
A harmony rich, where the heart's love grows

7. Footprints of Ancestors

Footprints in the sand,
Whispers of those who have walked,
Guiding us forward.

Paths worn with their strength,
Echoes of laughter and tears,
Carved in earth and time.

Memories tethered,
Family roots deep as roots,
Branches in the sky.

Silent stories told,
In the shadows of the past,
We carry them forth.

In each step we take,
Their legacy surrounds us,
Guides us through the night.

In the twilight glow,
Footprints fade but never cease,
Echoes of their past.

Ancient pathways lurk,
Beneath the weight of the years,
Each step a heartbeat.

Traditions woven,
In the fabric of our lives,
Stitched with love and hope.

Through meadows and woods,
Their stories intertwine ours,
Roots reach deep below.

Faded trails of joy,
Paths of struggle and resolve,
Lead us to their peace.

Each footprint a tale,
Carved in time, a silent guide,
Bringing us to light.

Long the journey traveled,
Across valleys, mountains high,
Their strength shapes our soul.

In the morning mist,
Footprints blend with dew-kissed grass,
Nature holds their dreams.

Whispers in the winds,
Carrying tales from the past,
Guiding our resolve.

Silent marbled stones,
Engraved with names and with love,
Honor those who came.

In the stars above,
Constellations of the past,
They watch over us.

Through laughter and pain,
Footprints etched in memory,
Bind us, heart to heart.

With each passing day,
Their spirit walks beside us,
Lighting up our way.

In shadows we walk,

Ancestors' voices call soft,
Roots entwined with fate.

17

8. Rivers of Beliefs

Beneath the vast canopy of stars,
where dreams intertwine with the dusk,
flow the rivers of beliefs—
liquid whispers of hope,
each current a narrative,
shaped by the hearts that yearn.

From the mountains of ancient wisdom,
they cascade,
clear and fierce,
carving valleys of understanding,
each bend a testimony to faith,
each ripple a question
that dances upon the surface.

In the placid pools,
where seekers pause to reflect,
ripples of compassion blend,
spilling over banks of tradition,
mingling with the silt of time—

an alchemy of thoughts and stories
that nourish the soul.

Some streams rush with fervor,
a torrent of fervent voices,
filling the air with passion,
while others meander gently,
the soft murmurs of quiet beliefs,
whispering secrets of the earth,
woven threads of unity,
binding us together.

Yet, amidst the flowing waters,
dissonance may surface,
clashing torrents against silent eddies,
a reminder that our rivers, though distinct,
feed into one great ocean—
the sea of human experience,
vast and infinite,
where depths remain uncharted,
and waves of empathy wash ashore.

So let us stand by the banks,
with open hearts and hands,
to drink from these rivers,
to share in their currents,
for in the gathering flows,

where beliefs converge,
we find not the end,
but the beginning of understanding,
the
promise of harmony
in the confluence of our lives.

9. Laughter across Languages

In the vibrant hues of India,
laughter blooms like marigolds,
a symphony of sounds,
each dialect a unique note,
humming through crowded lanes.

In the north, amidst the mountains,
"हंसी" dances on the lips,
twinkling in the eyes of children
who chase dreams like the fluttering flags,
while echoes carry through the valleys.

Down south, beneath the banyan shade,
"சிரிப்பு" flows like a gentle river,
soft and warm,
binding friends over cups of chai,
stories woven into the steam.

In the heart of Maharashtra,

"हसणे" roars like the ocean,
as laughter erupts in Ganeshotsav,
a vibrant wave crashing against mundane,
unifying souls in festive joy.

Eastward, where the horizon kisses the sea,
"হাসি" spills like the tide,
washing over fishermen and poets alike,
a collective cheer,
as the sun rises over Kolkata.

In the west, beneath the desert sky,
"હાસ્ય" rings out,
sprinkling warmth in every festival,
from Navratri to Diwali,
a celebration that transcends the stars.

Through languages, through cultures,
laughter becomes our common tongue,
an unspoken bond,
echoing in every corner,
celebrating the essence of being human.

So let us gather in this kaleidoscope,
where every laugh is a brushstroke,
painting a canvas vast and rich—
for in the laughter across India,

we find not just joy,
but the pulse of a nation,
beating with shared stories,
and the promise of togetherness

10. Melodies of Togetherness

In the symphony of life,
where voices softly blend,
we find the gentle chords of unity,
in every note, a friend.

The morning sun awakens,
with a tender, golden hue,
its rays like strings of violins,
binding skies of blue.

Chirping birds compose the dawn,
a chorus pure and bright,
their harmonies a promise shared,
in the fading night.

Through bustling streets and quiet lanes,
a melody unfolds,
in laughter shared and burdens eased,
a symphony that holds.

Across vast fields and cityscapes,
the rhythm of our hands,
working side by side in tune,
across these varied lands.

The gentle hum of whispered thoughts,
in twilight's calming glow,
connects the heartbeats of the world,
in music sweet and slow.

As evening brings its soft refrain,
beneath the starlit skies,
we dance to tunes of shared dreams,
with hope that never dies.

For in the melodies of togetherness,
life's true beauty gleams,
a song of unity and peace,
woven from our dreams.

May these notes forever linger,
in hearts and minds entwined,
the music of a world in harmony,
with love forever kind.

11. Brotherhood of togetherness

In the quiet morning light,
we gather, hearts aligned,
a circle formed by laughter,
a tapestry intertwined.

No need for grand gestures,
or declarations loud and bold,
for in the simplest moments,
true brotherhood unfolds.

Through storms and sunny days,
we share the weight we bear,
in whispers of encouragement,
in the strength of knowing care.

We grasp each other's hands,
as trials come our way,
a bond that knows no distance,
come what may.

With every step together,
we build a bridge anew,
for every heart that joins us,
makes this journey true.

Through the eyes of one another,
we find our stories blend,
a melody of togetherness,
in kinship without end.

When shadows start to lengthen,
and doubts begin to creep,
we stand as one in brotherhood,
waking dreams from sleep.

In laughter shared over fireside,
in silent moments spent,
the brotherhood we nurture,
is a love that's heaven-sent.

So here's to all the ties that bind,
and to the paths we tread,
in the brotherhood of togetherness,
we're stronger, hand in hand.

12. Dances of Seasons

In spring, the earth awakens,
with colors bright and bold,
the Bharatanatyam flows like rivers,
a story deftly told.
With intricate footwork dancing,
and grace in every line,
the blossoms sway in rhythm,
as nature starts to shine.

Summer brings the vibrant Bhangra,
as fields of gold abound,
with joyous leaps and hearty laughter,
the spirit dances round.
As the sun beats down with fervor,
celebrations fill the air,
in the pulse of every heartbeat,
there's a fervent love and care.

Then autumn wraps the world in orange,
and Kathak takes the stage,

twirling reams of flowing fabric,
as stories shift with age.
With spins that tell of seasons passed,
and gazes filled with grace,
the cool winds whisper tales of love,
as dancers find their place.

As winter's chill descends upon,
the earth in blankets white,
the Garba circles in the night,
a joyful, twinkling sight.
With clapping hands and swirling skirts,
and feet that tap with glee,
the warmth of community ignites,
in a tapestry so free.

In the stillness of the year's end,
the Odissi offers peace,
flowing like the sacred river,
in movements that don't cease.
With every pose, a prayer is sung,
to honor what has passed,
celebrating all the seasons,
in harmony, steadfast.

So through the cycles of the year,
these dances intertwine,

an ode to time and nature's grace,
each step, a link divine.
In every twirl and every leap,
the essence of life flows,
the dances of our seasons,
in hearts, forever glows.

13. Celebrating Common ground

In the mosaic of our differences,
where colors brightly blend,
we gather in the spirit of unity,
with open hearts, we mend.
Beneath the vast and endless sky,
our stories find their place,
woven through the threads of life,
each pattern holds a grace.

Through laughter shared and stories told,
we bridge the gaps of time,
as voices rise in harmony,
a melody, sublime.
From every walk of life we come,
with dreams both big and small,
in the garden of our common ground,
there's room for one and all.

Let cultures dance like autumn leaves,

in swirling, vibrant hues,
for in our varied ways of life,
there's so much we can choose.
To learn, to grow, to understand,
to celebrate the parts,
that bind us in the fabric's weave,
the beating of our hearts.

In the silence after storms have passed,
when shadows gently fade,
we'll find the beauty in our ties,
the moments that we've made.
With hands held tight, we'll rise as one,
embracing what we share,
for in the light of common ground,
we nurture love and care.

So let us break the chains of doubt,
and step beyond the walls,
to find our strength in unity,
and answer kindness' calls.
In the tapestry of human hearts,
may we forever stand,
a celebration of our common ground,
in peace, hand in hand.

14. Voices of village

At dawn, the rooster starts to sing,
the village stirs, a lively thing.
Footsteps echo on the stone,
the town awakens, never alone.

Underneath the ancient trees,
elders gather, sharing the breeze.
With weathered hands, they tell their tales,
of dreams that soared and ships that sailed.

Children's laughter, bright and wild,
in every corner, a curious child.
Their joy bursts forth like morning light,
a dance of shadows, pure delight.

Women chat near the bustling stand,
weaving their hopes with skilled hands.
Voices blend like colors bright,
that paint the canvas of day and night.

Men at work, with grit and pride,
building futures side by side.
In their chatter, strength reveals,
stories of hardship, hope that heals.

As the sun sinks low in the sky,
the village sings, a soft goodbye.
In every voice, a shared refrain—
the pulse of life, the village's gain.

15. Cradles of Culture

In hearths where echoes of old stories lie,
The cradle rocks with whispers, soft and slow,
From every craft and dance, the spirits fly,
In vibrant hues where ancient rivers flow.

The potter's wheel spins tales of earth and fire,
As hands mold clay with wisdom, age-defined,
Each painted pot reflects a deep desire,
To carry forth the legacy entwined.

The rhythm of the drums beneath the moon,
A dance of feet upon the sacred ground,
Each step, a heartbeat, forming a commune,
Where history and hope in harmony abound.

In twilight hours, the storytellers come,
With voices rich as honey, sweet and deep,
They weave the past, till silence feels like hum,
And every listener, in rapture, weeps.

In language born of struggle, laughter, pain,
Words flow like rivers, carving through the stone,
Each dialect a thread in culture's chain,
A symbol of the battles won alone.

The artisans with skillful hands create,
Intricate designs that speak of home and pride,
From textiles bright to sculptures that await,
In every piece, the heartbeats coincide.

The flavors mixed in kitchens rich and bold,
Spices dance upon the air, a fragrant song,
Recipes passed from the young to the old,
Each dish a tale of where the soul belongs.

In every festival that lights the night,
With lanterns soaring high, they bridge the years,
Traditions glow, a tapestry of light,
Uniting all in joy and shared cheers.

So let us cherish these cradles of grace,
A chorus of voices, a heritage's love,
For in their arms, the world finds its place,
A tapestry of life, woven from above.

16. Dance of Divinity

In moonlit night where shadows softly play,
The stars awaken to a sacred tune,
A rhythm felt in every heart's array,
The dance of divinity beneath the moon.

With graceful steps, the cosmos takes its flight,
Galaxies twirl like partners in embrace,
Each spark of light ignites the velvet night,
In every twirl, a glimpse of timeless grace.

The whispers of the ancients in the breeze,
As earth and sky in harmony align,
The rustling leaves and swaying, bending trees,
Each movement speaks of love that dares to shine.

From sacred temples, echoes of the past,
Where deities in marble rise and fall,
Their stories etched in stone, forever cast,
In every dance, they hear our yearning call.

The rivers flow, a current soft and bold,
Each drop a note in nature's grand ballet,
While mountains stand as guardians of old,
Their strength a rhythm in the dance of day.

In every flutter of a butterfly,
In every child's laughter, pure and bright,
The spirit sways beneath a boundless sky,
Inviting all to join this sacred rite.

So let us dance, with arms wide open, free,
With every heartbeat, let our souls entwine,
In the dance of divinity, we see
A unity that's written in the divine.

For in this dance, we find our truest form,
As love and light embrace the evening's grace,
Together spinning, bending, rising warm,
In the eternal waltz, we find our place.

17. Ceremonies under the sky

Beneath the arch of endless azure blue,
Where whispers of the wind carry our dreams,
We gather 'neath the sacred, vast debut,
To honor life with laughter, love, and schemes.

The sun, a golden witness to our rites,
Casts shimmering blessings on our bare feet,
As hearts unite like stars in distant nights,
Together, we create a rhythm sweet.

With open hands, we offer up our words,
In prayers that rise like smoke from sacred fires,
Each note of gratitude, like songs of birds,
A tapestry of hopes, of joys, desires.

The earth beneath, a canvas for our feet,
As dancers weave their stories in the dust,
In every heartbeat, ancient echoes meet,
And timeless energies blend into trust.

With vibrant colors painted on the skin,
We mark our passage through the circle's grace,
Each symbol wrapped in meaning from within,
In unity, we find our sacred space.

As twilight whispers secrets to the night,
The stars above ignite our collective eye,
Illuminating paths with gentle light,
A constellation of our dreams up high.

And in the hush that follows every cheer,
We feel the pulse of life, both fierce and kind,
In every gathering, the loved ones near,
We forge connections that the heavens bind.

So let us gather, under sky so wide,
In ceremonies woven with each breath,
With joy, we stand, our spirits amplified,
In every moment, celebrating life's breadth.

18. Cuisines of Connection

In kitchens bright across the land we find,
A tapestry of flavors, diverse and intertwined.

From North to South, East to West they spread,
Each region's bounty, a story to be fed.

In the North, rich butter chicken glistens bright,
And naan embraces warmth on cold winter nights.

Chaat from the streets, a festival of zest,
With tangy tamarind, it captivates each guest.

Eastward, Bengali fish, in mustard sautéed,
And sweets like rasgulla, where joy is lovingly laid.

From the hills of Assam, fragrant tea does flow,
In every sip, a piece of heritage we know.

Southward, dosa and idli grace the plate,
Coconut chutney serves to celebrate.

Sambar bubbling gently, a spice-laden brew,
In every home, it whispers, "Welcome to anew."

And in the West, where spices make their mark,
Puran poli and dhokla, igniting every spark.

Saffron and cardamom weave their tales so sweet,
In every thali, a journey, a taste, a heartbeat.

Goa's seafood dances on the shores of the sea,
With flavors that sing of sun and harmony.

Across the land, from coast to vibrant coast,
Food builds our connections, something we all boast.

Each meal a gathering, each dish a shared delight,
Uniting hearts and hands, in love's warm, gentle light.

In every bite, respect for culture holds,
A unity of flavors, a connection that unfolds.

So let us celebrate this culinary art,
For in every cuisine, beats India's heart.

19. Stories carved in stone

In the heart of India, where silence speaks,
Ancient stones hold secrets as time runs deep.
Temples stand tall, like guardians of the past,
Whispering tales of glory, that forever will last.

From Hampi's ruins, where kings once did reign,
Echoes of power, of triumphs, and pain.
Coronation ceremonies, where pride would not hide,
In murals and statues, the spirits confide.

In the embrace of Khajuraho, passion finds form,
Figures entwined, in a dance that's warm.
Sculptures of ecstasy, captured mid-flow,
Expressions of love in the stone's gentle glow.

The love of a king, in marble so bright,
The Taj Mahal gleams, a beacon in the night.
A testament to devotion, carved with such care,
Love immortalized, a story laid bare.

In the hills of Mahabalipuram, waves softly crash,
As artisans etch legends with a formidable splash.
The Shore Temple stands, kissed by the sea,
Telling stories of sailors, of journeys so free.

In the ancient caves of Ajanta, visions delight,
Buddha's serene gaze, a halo of light.
Carved with precision, tales of his quest,
Paths of enlightenment that never find rest.

The intricate patterns of the Sun Temple's grace,
Reflecting the cosmos, a celestial space.
Each stone a chapter, each corner a tale,
Of sun worshipers dancing, their spirits set sail.

In the forests of Kanheri, wisdom takes flight,
Buddha in the rock, glowing with tranquil light.
Sculpted in serenity, a path to the soul,
Stories of peace, where the heart can console.

And as we wander, through history's embrace,
These stories carved in stone, a cultural trace.
A tapestry woven of time, place, and grace,
In every etched fragment, a memory we face.

So let us honor these relics, where echoes remain,
For they speak of our journey, our joy, and our pain.

In India's embrace, let their stories be known,
For amidst life's transience, they stand as our own.

20. Unity in mosaic

In a world of colors, bright and bold,
Each tiny piece carries a story untold.
Jagged edges, smooth and round,
Together they whisper, a harmony found.

Fragments of glass, tiles in array,
Diverse and distinct, they dance in display.
A mosaic of cultures, beliefs intertwined,
In unity's cradle, a vision defined.

Shattered pieces, once cast aside,
Now joined together, with love as their guide.
Each hue a heartbeat, every shade a voice,
In this vibrant canvas, we celebrate choice.

Crimson for passion, azure for peace,
Golden for hope, where divisions cease.
Every color reflects a unique point of view,
Yet in their togetherness, they bloom anew.

Through trials and storms, the mosaic stays strong,
A testament to resilience, where all belong.
No single tile claims the glory or fame,
For unity whispers, "We're all the same."

As we walk through this life, let us remember the art,
Of merging our pieces, of playing our part.
In the grand tapestry, let compassion be found,
For in unity's mosaic, true beauty is crowned.

21. India - my heart

In the cradle of time, where the rivers weave,
A land of dreams, in beauty we believe.
From the snowy peaks, where the eagles soar,
To the verdant plains and the ocean's roar.

Golden fields of mustard, stretching far and wide,
Whispers of history in the Ganges tide.
Beneath the Banyan, where sages once sat,
Echoes of wisdom in the heart of our mat.

A symphony of languages, a chorus of tongues,
In the marketplace chatter, where each story hums.
From the songs of the Punjabi to the Tamil's grace,
India's essence blooms in each sacred space.

The vibrant festivals adorn every street,
Diwali's light and Eid's blessed greet.
Holi's colors dance on the canvas of skin,
A celebration of life, where unity begins.

In the busy bazaars, where aromas collide,
Spices and textiles, a cultural tide.
Hands that craft stories in every design,
Where the threads of our heritage magnificently
intertwine.

Through the corridors of time, our struggle endured,
From the warriors of yore to freedom's assured.
In the spirit of Gandhi, a vision so bright,
Of peace and of strength, a guiding light.

Under the Tricolor, we stand hand in hand,
A mosaic of voices, a diverse, vibrant land.
In every heart beats a dream of the whole,
A vision of growth, a collective goal.

The mountains may rise and the rivers may flow,
But the heart of India, it endlessly glows.
With rhythms of folk in each village square,
In the tapestry woven is a brotherhood rare.

Let's celebrate each hue, each unique strand,
For together we flourish, together we stand.
In the symphony of this epic refrain,
Unity in diversity—a powerful gain.

So here's to the spirit that soars like a kite,

In the land of our birth, where futures shine bright.
With courage as our pillar and love as our art,
In the tapestry of India, beats a singular heart.